100 Based Weird & Trivia Facts About Baseball For
Gen Z, Millennials, Gen X, Baby Boomers & All Generations

100 BASED FACTS ABOUT BASEBALL

© 2024

This based book of facts belongs to:

FOREWORD

Change is constant. All based facts on baseball have a chance to change over time – and many could be disputed. Feel free to update these facts and add your own notes.

Have fun and PLAY BALL!

#1

In March 2001, pitcher Randy Johnson hit a dove with a fastball during a spring season game. The bird did not make it.

#2

The pitch that hit the bird was called a "no pitch" and did not count.

#3

Most people know it is 90 ft in between bases, but with the size of bases being 18 in, the distance between is actually 87 ft (home plate to 1st or 3rd) and 87 ft, 9 in. (between 1st, 2nd, 3rd base).

#4

A regular baseball has 108 double stitches, or 216 single stitches.

100 Based Facts About Baseball

#5

The average 9-inning baseball game is about 3 hours long, though it dropped to 2 hours 40 minutes in 2023.

#6

The quickest 9-inning baseball was supposedly 51 minutes back in 1919.

#7

Baseball is the only professional major league sport that has no time limit.

#8

The Dodgers team name came from people having to dodge the Brooklyn trolleys in front of the ball park.

100 Based Facts About Baseball

#9

The shortest player ever appearing in a game was Eddie Gaedel, who stood at 3 ft, 7 in for the St. Louis Browns in 1951.

#10

The tallest player ever appearing in a game was Jon Rauch, who stands at 7 ft. 1 in, for the Chicago White Sox in 2002.

#11

There has only been one perfect game in the World Series and playoffs, thrown by Don Larsen in 1956.

#12

No pitcher in professional baseball history has thrown more than one perfect game in their career.

#13

The Philadelphia Phillies are the oldest same name, same city, continuous franchise in baseball history.

#14

The word base-ball first appeared in England in a 1744 children's book.

#15

Baseball was an Olympic demonstration sport five times in 1912, 1936, 1956, 1964, and 1984.

#16

Baseball was an official Olympic sport from 1992 until 2008 when it was discontinued.

#17

The fastest pitch ever recorded was thrown by Aroldis Chapman in 2010, and was clocked at 105.8 mph.

The slowest pitch in baseball is called the eephus pitch, a slow, high-arc baseball that can go around 30 mph.

#19

There have been over 60 players who hit a home run in their final at bat, but only two Hall of Famers: Mickey Cochrane and Ted Williams.

#20

The term "bullpen" first appeared for baseball in 1877 as fans in standing room only areas had to be herded like cattle.

#21

The infield fly rule was first introduced in 1895 and amended twice to exclude line drives and bunt attempts.

#22

Baseball was an official Olympic sport from 1992 until 2008 when it was discontinued.

#23

The first Major League Baseball team
was the Cincinnati Red Stockings.

#24

The first baseball major league team to
move cities was the Milwaukee Brewers
who became the St. Louis Browns in
1901.

#25

The balk rule was first introduced in 1898.

The most balks committed in one game was 5, committed by Bob Shaw in 1963.

#27

The first father and son to play for the same team were Ken Griffey, Sr. and Ken Griffey Jr., in 1990.

#28

On September 14, 1990, the Griffey father and son duo hit back-to-back home runs.

#29

There have been over 300 no-hitters in baseball history and over 20 perfect games.

#30

There have been 6 teams to throw no hitters and still lose the games.

#31

The song "Take Me Out to the Ballgame" was first performed at a high school baseball game in 1937.

#32

The composers of "Take Me Out to the Ballgame" - Jack Norwith and Albert Von Tilzer – had never seen a baseball game when they wrote the song.

#33

During the Civil War there were two primary types of baseball: Massachusetts baseball used a soft ball, and New York baseball used a hard ball.

#34

During World War II, over 500 major league players left baseball and joined the armed services.

#35

The oldest minor league team name is the Buffalo Bisons, dating back to 1877.

#36

The Atlanta Braves baseball club is the oldest team, originally founded as the Boston Red Stockings in 1871.

#37

While rain delays are common, Game 3 of the 1989 World Series was delayed and postponed due to an earthquake as the teams were warming up to start the game.

#38

Game 2 of the 2007 American League Championship Series saw a slight pause in a baseball game due to a swarm of bugs called midges.

#39

Astroturf, named for its application at the Houston Astros stadium, was originally called ChemGrass.

#40

The Astros are named to recognize the Houston area NASA Space Center, but were previously called the Colt .45's.

#41

The first U.S. President to throw out a first pitch was William Howard Taft in 1910.

#42

In 2015, Evelyn Jones became the oldest person to throw out a first pitch at 108 years old.

100 Based Facts About Baseball

#43

The Oakland Athletics had a player called Coco Crisp, although his real first name was Covelli.

#44

Richard "Goose" Gossage got his nickname from a friend who did not like the nickname "Goss" and said he had a long neck like a goose.

#45

Satchel Paige became the oldest player to play in the major leagues at 59 years and 80 days old.

#46

Three months after Jackie Robinson broke the color barrier in 1947, Larry Doby of the Cleveland Indians because the second black player in the majors, and the first in the American League.

100 Based Facts About Baseball

#47

The highest batting average in one season is Nap Lajoie's .426, which he achieved in 1901.

BETTER THAN AVERAGE

#48

The highest batting average for a career goes to Ty Cobb, with a .366 batting average over 24 seasons.

#49

In 2023, pitcher Shohei Ohtani became the first person since Babe Ruth for the most strikeouts thrown in a season for a player with at least 100 home runs.

#50

In the late 1800's, bad baseball players became known as "muffins" because they would "muff" the ball.

#51

Peck and Snyder, a sporting goods store, is considered to have created the first baseball cards in 1868, although players had photo cards produced by teams prior.

#52

The most expensive baseball card in the world to date is the Mickey Mantle 1952 Topps card that sold for $12.6 million in 2022.

100 Based Facts About Baseball

#53

Stealing bases became allowed in baseball in 1898.

#54

The highest number of bases stolen in one season is 138, set in 1887 by Hugh Nicol.

100 Based Facts About Baseball

#55

"Louisville Slugger" is not just the name of the bat, it was originally the nickname of Hall of Famer Pete Browning.

#56

Most major league baseball bats (75%) are made from maple wood, with ash and birch woods making up the next most common types of wood.

#57

The longest game of baseball was 26 innings, between the Brooklyn Robins and Boston Braves in 1920.

#58

The game above was ended after 3 hours and 50 minutes because night fell.

100 Based Facts About Baseball

#59

The first night major league game was played May 24, 1935 in Cincinnati.

#60

President Franklin Delano Roosevelt threw the "opening switch" to turn on the lights for that first night game.

100 Based Facts About Baseball

#61

The most common grass found on major league fields is Kentucky Bluegrass.

#62

The soil that is used for most major league baseball fields is made up of about half sand, then clay and silt.

#63

Only 3 teams in the major league do not have mascots: Angels, Dodgers, and Yankees.

#64

Of all the current mascots in the major leagues, only one is a dinosaur: Dinger the triceratops for the Colorado Rockies.

#65

The first baseball team in Japan was formed in 1878.

#66

Japanese baseball allows for ties, and has a 12-inning limit during the regular season and 15-inning limit in the playoffs.

100 Based Facts About Baseball

#67

The squeeze play was supposedly invented in 1894 at a Yale University ball game.

#68

The Designated Hitter position was adopted in 1973 by the American League and later by the National League in 2022.

100 Based Facts About Baseball

#69

The baseball park at the highest elevation is Colorado's Coors Field, at a 5,211 ft. above sea level.

#70

According to scientists, baseballs hit at Coors Field are likely to travel 10% farther than at lower elevation parks.

#71

Former Manager Bobby Cox holds the record for the most times ejected during a career – he was ejected from 162 games.

#72

The umpire who ejected the most people throughout his career was Hall of Famer Bill Klem, who ejected 251 players during his career.

#73

The Dodgers sell more hot dogs in a baseball season than any other teams, selling around 2.5 million "Dodger Dogs."

#74

Hot dogs remain among the most popular food item in major league parks, apart from Milwaukee, where it is bratwurst.

#75

The youngest major league baseball player ever to play was Joe Nuxhall who debuted for Cincinnati in 1944 at 15 years and 10 months old.

#76

On June 15, 1976 there was a game rainout at the Houston Astrodome due to heavy rains and flooding around the dome, despite the teams both being at the park and ready to play.

#77

The former Montreal Expos team was named after the Expo 1967 World's Fair that was held in Montreal – it was also spelled the same in French and English.

#78

If you count Brooklyn, New York City has had four major league baseball teams over time: Giants, Dodgers, Yankees, and Mets.

#79

The New York Yankees have the greatest number of World Series wins at 27.

#80

There are five teams that have never won the World Series: Milwaukee, Tampa Bay, Colorado, San Diego, and Seattle.

#81

Hughie Jennings, who played and managed baseball from 1891 to 1925, was hit by a league record 287 pitches during his career.

#82

Pitcher Gus Weyhing holds the career record for having hit 277 batters during his career from 1887 to 1901.

#83

In 1999, Manager Bobby Valentine was ejected from a game, and later slipped back into the dugout wearing a disguise that included a mustache – he was later fined.

#84

The biggest comeback in baseball history happened in 2001 when the Seattle Mariners trailed the Cleveland Indians 14-2 entering the bottom of the 7th inning. They ended up winning 15-14.

#85

The highest scoring baseball game happened in 1922 when the Chicago Cubs beat the Philadelphia Phillies 26-23.

#86

The most runs scored by one team were 36 runs by the Chicago Colts in 1897 – the modern era record is 30 runs in one game by the Texas Rangers in 2007.

#87

Nolan Ryan is not only the career strikeout record leader with 5,714 strikeouts, but he also has a record 7 no-hitters.

#88

Three pitchers share the single game strikeout record with 20 strikeouts: Max Scherzer, Kerry Wood, and Roger Clemens (who did it twice).

100 Based Facts About Baseball

#89

The letter "K" is used to designate a strikeout because the first four letters were already used to designate other baseball actions.

It's short for strikeout.

#90

Bill Keister of the Baltimore Orioles holds the record for most errors in a single season, committing 97 errors in 1901.

#91

The rarest play in baseball is the unassisted triple play – it has only happened 15 times in over 100 years.

#92

Winning the hitting triple crown in a season – leading the league in batting average, home runs, and RBIs – has only happened 17 times, with the last time in 2012 by Miguel Cabrera.

#93

Four times in baseball history, a team has committed 3 errors on the same single play with the most recent happening in 2014 by the Los Angeles Dodgers.

#94

In May of 2012, Jamie Moyer became the oldest pitcher – at 49 years and 151 days old - to have won a baseball game.

#95

The highest attended game in baseball history was a 2008 preseason game at the Los Angeles Coliseum, between the Dodgers and Boston Red Sox: 115,301 people attended.

#96

The least attended game in baseball history happened in 1882 between the Troy Trojans and the Worcesters, where 6 people allegedly attended.

#97

The first released baseball video game was Atari's Home Run, which was released in 1978 for the Atari VCS, later known as the Atari 2600.

#98

In 1993, pitcher Jim Abbott of the New York Yankees threw a no-hitter – Jim was born without a right hand.

#99

The All-American Girls Professional Baseball League existed for 9 years and was featured in the 1992 film *A League of Their Own.*

#100

It was the New York Mercury newspaper that reported baseball as the "National Pastime" in 1856.

Thank you!

We hoped you enjoyed these 100 Based Facts About Baseball - thank you for reading, and now….**PLAY BALL**!

100 Based Facts About Baseball

What were your favorite based facts?

100 Based Facts About Baseball

Made in United States
North Haven, CT
03 January 2025